At Sylvan, we believe reading is one of life's most important and enriching abilities, and we're glad you've chosen our resources to help your child build these critically important skills. We know that the time you spend with your child reinforcing the lessons learned in school will contribute to his love of reading. This love of reading will translate into academic achievement. A successful reader is ready for the world around him, ready to do research, ready to experience the world of literature, and prepared to make the connections necessary to achieve in school and in life.

We use a research-based, step-by-step process in teaching reading at Sylvan that includes thought-provoking reading selections and activities. As students increase their success as readers they become more confident. With increasing confidence, students build even more success. Our Sylvan workbooks are designed to help you to help your child build the skills and confidence that will contribute to your child's success in school.

We're excited to partner with you to support the development of a confident, well-prepared independent learner!

*The Sylvan Team*

# Sylvan Learning Center.
# Unleash your child's potential here.

No matter how big or small the academic challenge, every child has the ability to learn. But sometimes children need help making it happen. Sylvan believes every child has the potential to do great things. And we know better than anyone else how to tap into that academic potential so that a child's future really is full of possibilities. Sylvan Learning Center is the place where your child can build and master the learning skills needed to succeed and unlock the potential you know is there.

The proven, personalized approach of our in-center programs deliver unparalleled results that other supplemental education services simply can't match. Your child's achievements will be seen not only in test scores and report cards but outside the classroom as well. And when he starts achieving his full potential, everyone will know it. You will see a new level of confidence come through in everything he does and every interaction he has.

How can Sylvan's personalized in-center approach help your child unleash his potential?

- Starting with our exclusive Sylvan Skills Assessment®, we pinpoint your child's exact academic needs.

- Then we develop a customized learning plan designed to achieve your child's academic goals.

- Through our method of skill mastery, your child will not only learn and master every skill in his personalized plan, he will be truly motivated and inspired to achieve his full potential.

To get started, simply contact your local Sylvan Learning Center to set up an appointment. And to learn more about Sylvan and our innovative in-center programs, call 1-800-EDUCATE or visit www.SylvanLearning.com. *With over 850 locations in North America, there is a Sylvan Learning Center near you!*

# 1st Grade
# Reading Skill Builders
# Workbook

Published in the United States by Random House, Inc., New York, and in Canada by Random House of Canada Limited, Toronto.

www.sylvanlearning.com

Created by Smarterville Productions LLC
Producer: TJ Trochlil McGreevy
Producer & Editorial Direction: The Linguistic Edge
Writer: Christina Roll
Cover and Interior Illustrations: Duendes del Sur
Layout and Art Direction: SunDried Penguin
Art Manager: Adina Ficano

First Edition

ISBN: 978-0-375-43023-7

Library of Congress Cataloging-in-Publication Data available upon request.

This book is available at special discounts for bulk purchases for sales promotions or premiums. For more information, write to Special Markets/Premium Sales, 1745 Broadway, MD 6-2, New York, New York 10019 or e-mail specialmarkets@randomhouse.com.

PRINTED IN CHINA

# Contents

# Beginning Sounds

## Starting Line

SAY the name of each picture and LISTEN to its beginning sound. WRITE the letter to complete each word. Then READ each word out loud.

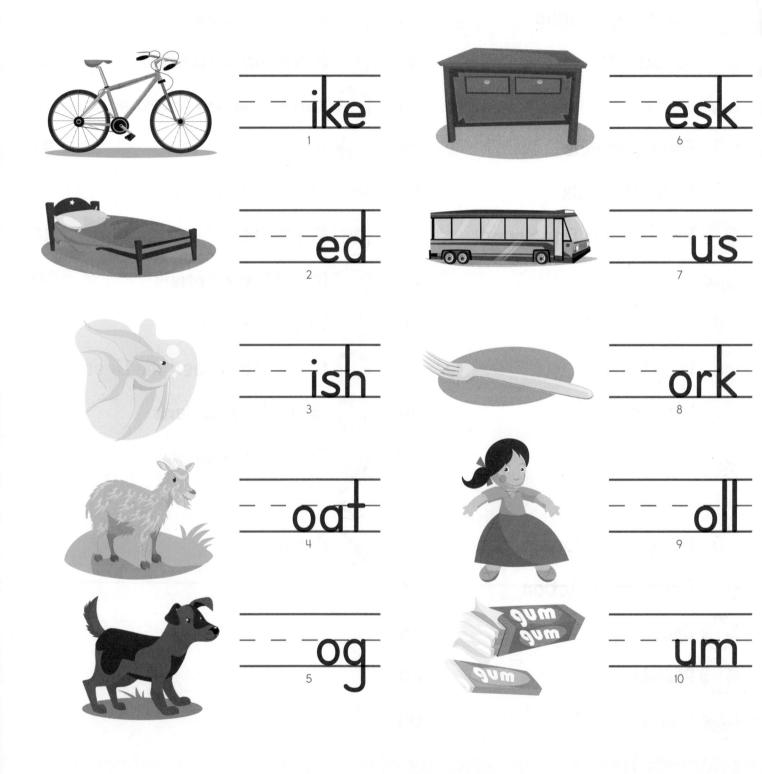

1. ike
2. ed
3. ish
4. oat
5. og
6. esk
7. us
8. ork
9. oll
10. um

## Maze Crazy!

Help the bee get to the hive. DRAW a line through the maze to connect the pictures whose names begin with the **b**, **d**, or **f** sound.

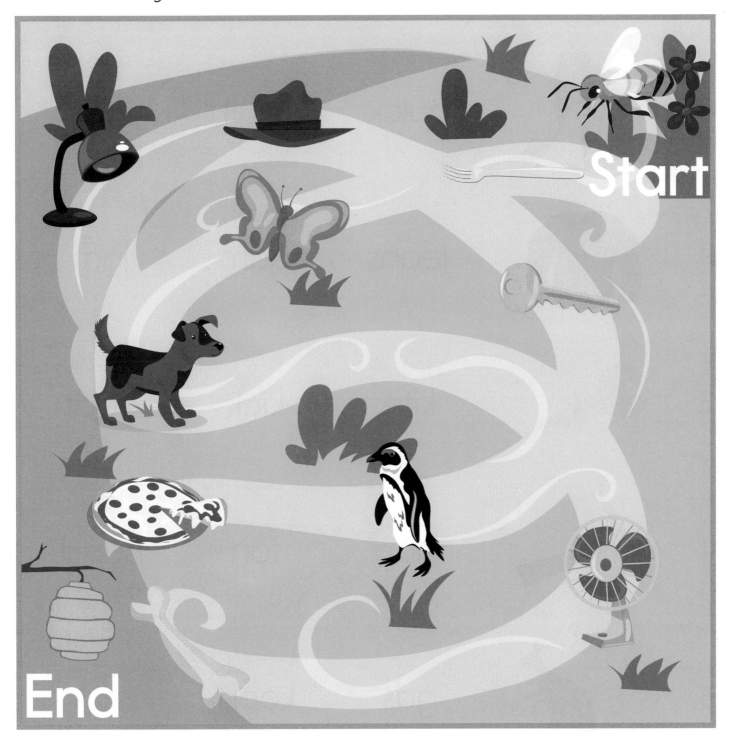

# Beginning Sounds

## Sounds and Words

SAY the name of the picture in each row and LISTEN to its beginning sound. CIRCLE the word or words in the row that have the same beginning sound.

1. quick     quit     fun

2. jeans     gum     jam

3. kite     kick     goat

4. mop     fan     hand

5. gas     keep     zip

## What's My Word?

SAY the name of each picture. CIRCLE the word that matches the picture.

1. hand    jam

2. rang    king

3. queen    nail

4. jump    jar

5. kite    tent

6. girl    quilt

7. hat    fall

8. jug    key

## What Starts My Name?

SAY the name of each picture. WRITE the correct word for each picture under the letter that makes its beginning sound. LOOK at the word box for help.

leaf    net    pan    mop    pig    log    mat    ~~nose~~

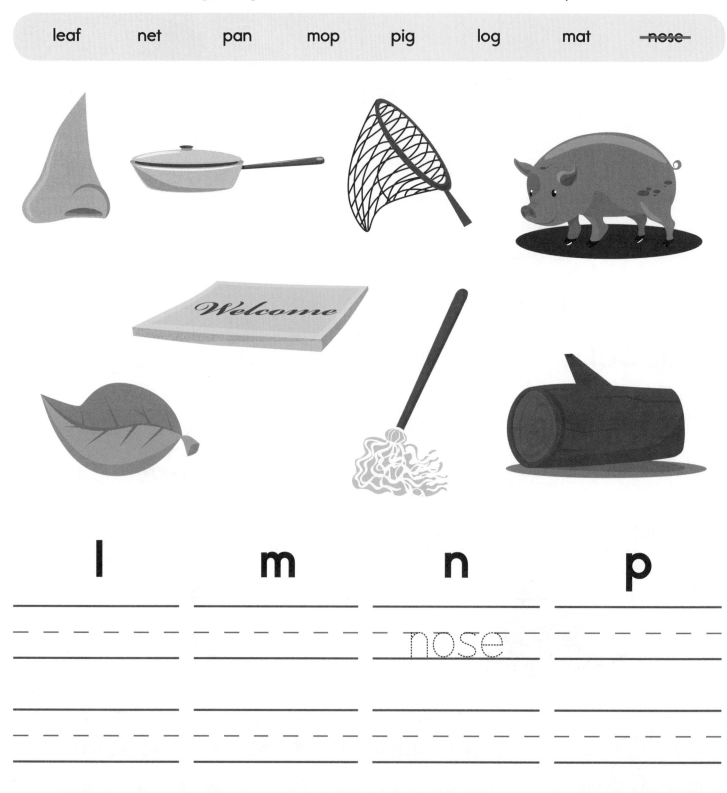

| l | m | n | p |
|---|---|---|---|
|   |   | nose |   |

## Picture Match

READ each sentence and FIND the matching picture. WRITE the correct number in the box.

1. I see a ladybug on a leaf.
2. The milk is on the mat.
3. The nest is next to the net.
4. I ate pizza and pie for lunch.

## Starting Line

SAY the name of each picture and LISTEN to its beginning sound. WRITE the letter to complete each word. Then READ each word out loud.

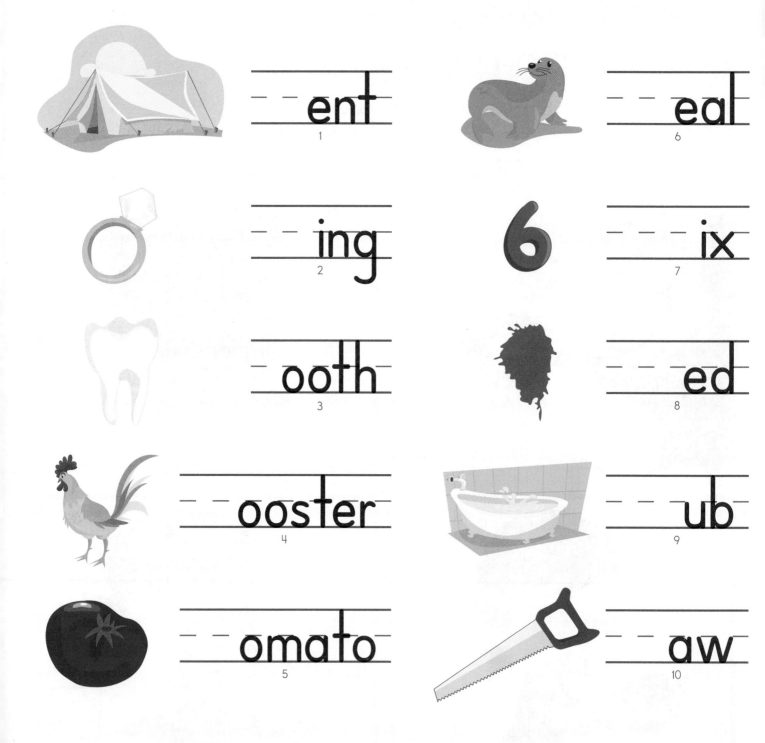

1. ent
2. ing
3. ooth
4. ooster
5. omato
6. eal
7. ix
8. ed
9. ub
10. aw

## Double Cross

SAY the name of each picture and LISTEN to its beginning sound. DRAW a line from each picture to its name.

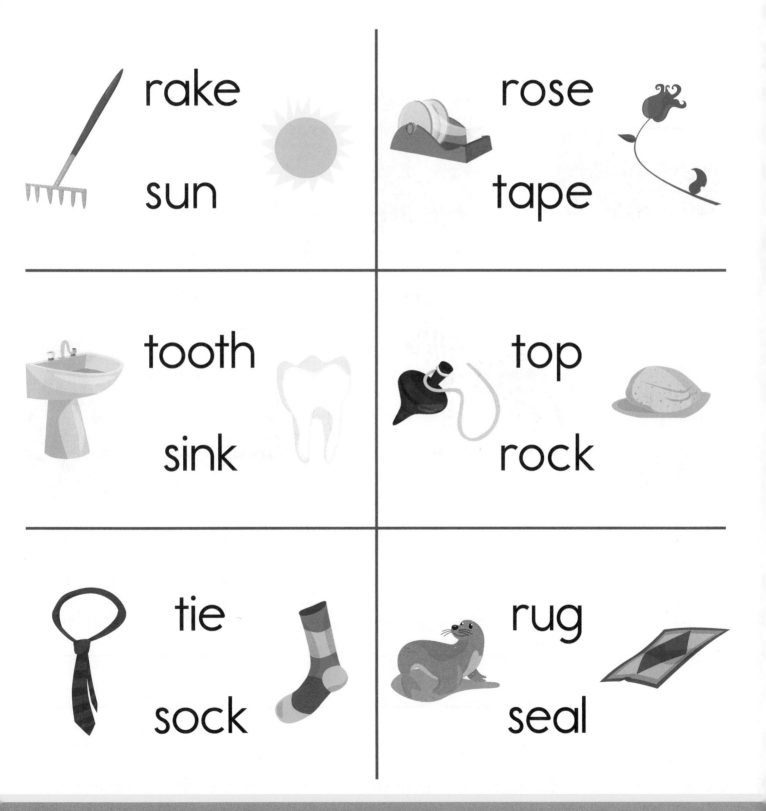

rake

sun

rose

tape

tooth

sink

top

rock

tie

sock

rug

seal

# Beginning Sounds

## What Starts My Name?

SAY the name of each picture. WRITE the correct word for each picture under the letter that makes its beginning sound. LOOK at the word box for help.

| zipper | van | wig | yo-yo | web | yellow | vase | zebra |

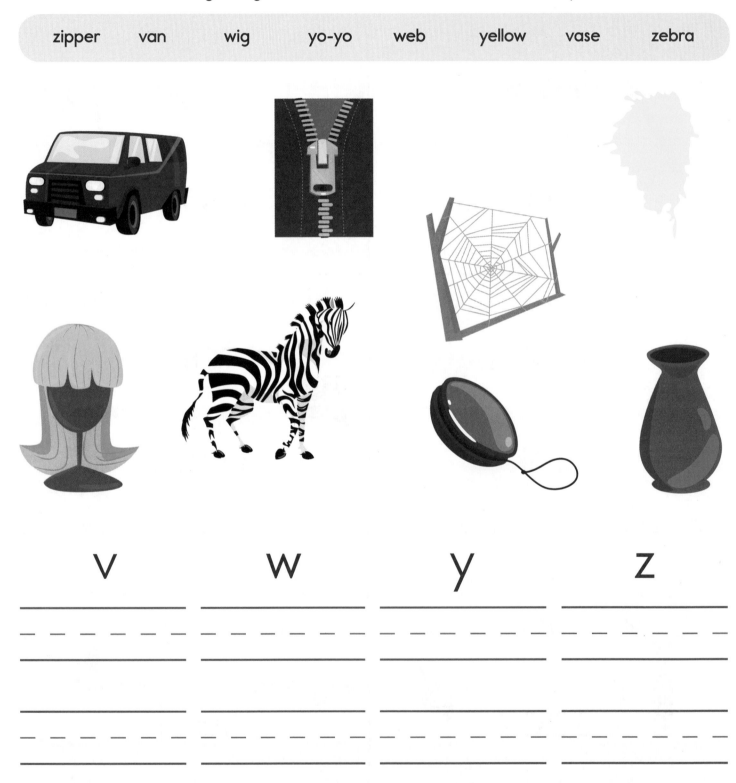

V

W

y

Z

## Word Connection

SAY the name of the picture. CIRCLE the letters that make its name. WRITE the word. Then READ the word out loud.

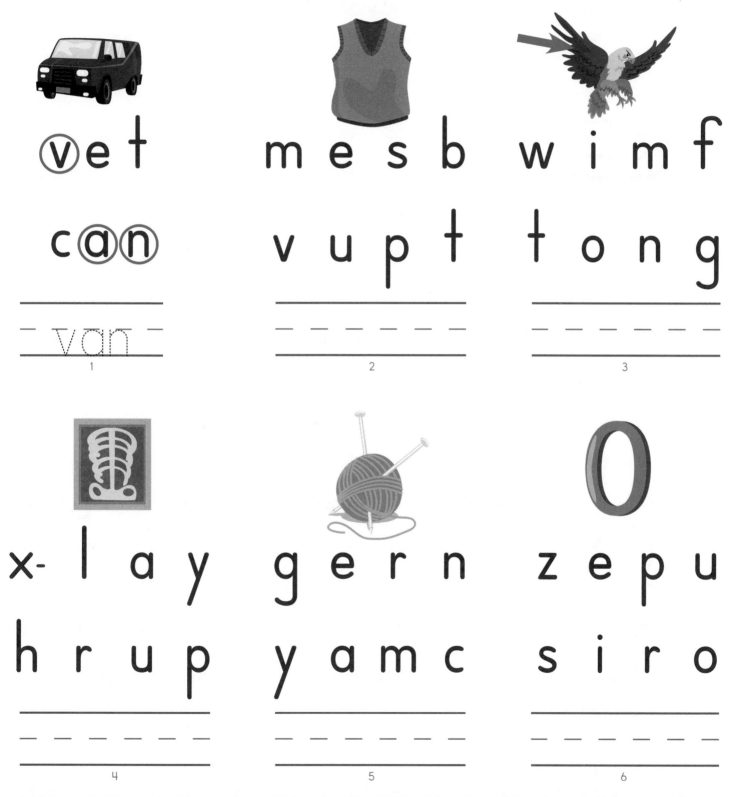

(v) e t

c (a) (n)

_van_
1

m e s b

v u p t

2

w i m f

t o n g

3

x- l a y

h r u p

4

g e r n

y a m c

5

z e p u

s i r o

6

## Circle It

The letter "c" has two sounds: **k** as in *coat* and **s** as in *city*.

The letter "g" also has two sounds: **g** as in *gold* and **j** as in *giant*.

SAY the name of the picture in each row. CIRCLE the word or words in the row that have the same beginning sound.

1.    kid      bed      hat      cage

2.    mail      cent      dog      sip

3.    get      give      nut      pop

4.    fish      jump      gem      queen

## Picture Match

READ each sentence and FIND the matching picture. WRITE the correct number in the box.

1. The cat and cow are in the garden.

2. Look at that giant cake!

3. The goat ate corn and carrots.

4. A girl took a cab to the city.

# Hide and Seek

READ the words in the word box. LOOK for the matching objects in the picture and CIRCLE them.

bed    desk    vase    kite    fan    yarn    lamp    dog    sock    rug

## Picture Match

CIRCLE the sentence that matches the picture.

**1.**

The cat is on the bed.

The cat is on the desk.

**2.**

The pig is in the mud.

The pig sits on a log.

**3.**

The queen eats ham.

The queen flies a kite.

**4.**

The zebra is on a ship.

The zebra wears a wig.

# Ending Sounds

## Finish Line

SAY the name of each picture and LISTEN to its ending sound. WRITE the letter to complete each word. Then READ each word out loud.

re __
1

su __
2

mo __
3

dru __
4

fa __
5

han __
6

cri __
7

ra __
8

to __
9

moo __
10

## Circle It

SAY the name of the picture in each row. CIRCLE the word or words in the row that have the same ending sound.

1.      gum      bird      clam

2.      seed      moon      log

3.      food      sad      wig

4.      jump      hook      top

5.      fix      rub      jet

# Ending Sounds

## Word Connection

SAY the name of the picture. CIRCLE the letters that make its name. WRITE the word. Then READ the word out loud.

geak

boet

_____

- - - - - - - -

_____

1

basl

fels

_____

- - - - - - - -

_____

2

shag

flip

_____

- - - - - - - -

_____

3

prett

dlass

_____

- - - - - - - -

_____

4

fatn

bork

_____

- - - - - - - -

_____

5

## Double Cross

SAY the name of each picture and LISTEN to its ending sound. DRAW a line from each picture to its name.

nut

bag

nail

duck

bus

net

shell

clock

gift

doll

gas

pig

## Stuck in the Middle

SAY the name of each picture and LISTEN to its middle sound. WRITE the letter or letters to complete each word. Then READ each word out loud.

HINT: You may need to add more than one letter to some words.

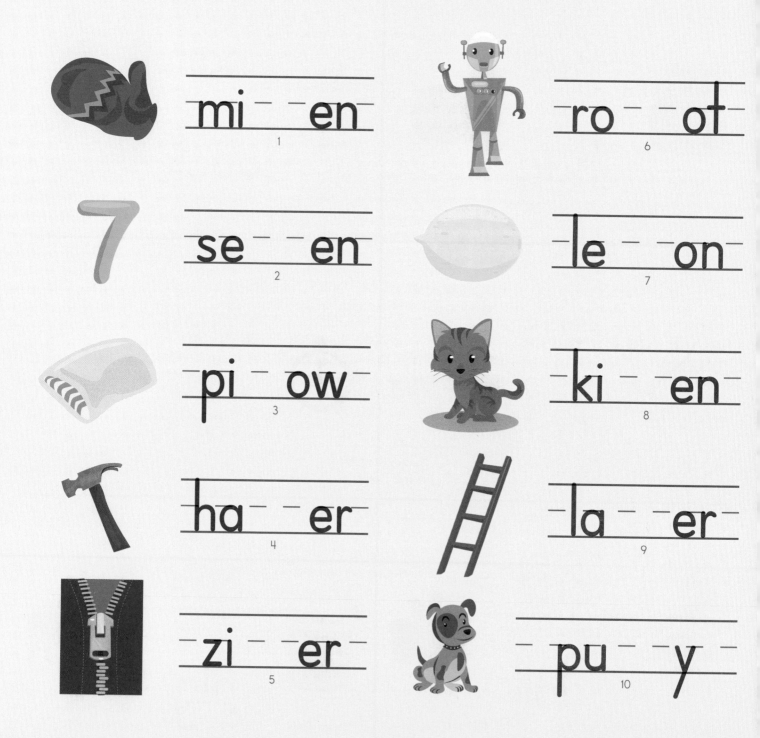

mi __ en
1

ro __ ot
6

se __ en
2

le __ on
7

pi __ ow
3

ki __ en
8

ha __ er
4

la __ er
9

zi __ er
5

pu __ y
10

## Circle It

SAY the name of the picture in each row and LISTEN to its middle sound. CIRCLE the word or words in the row that have the same middle sound.

1. pepper    metal    carrot

2. jacket    dinner    lizard

3. spider    wizard    hammer

4. muffin    ticket    jelly

5. parrot    wagon    chicken

# Two Letters, One Sound!

## Starting Line

SAY the name of each picture and LISTEN to its beginning sound. WRITE the letters to complete each word. Then READ each word out loud.

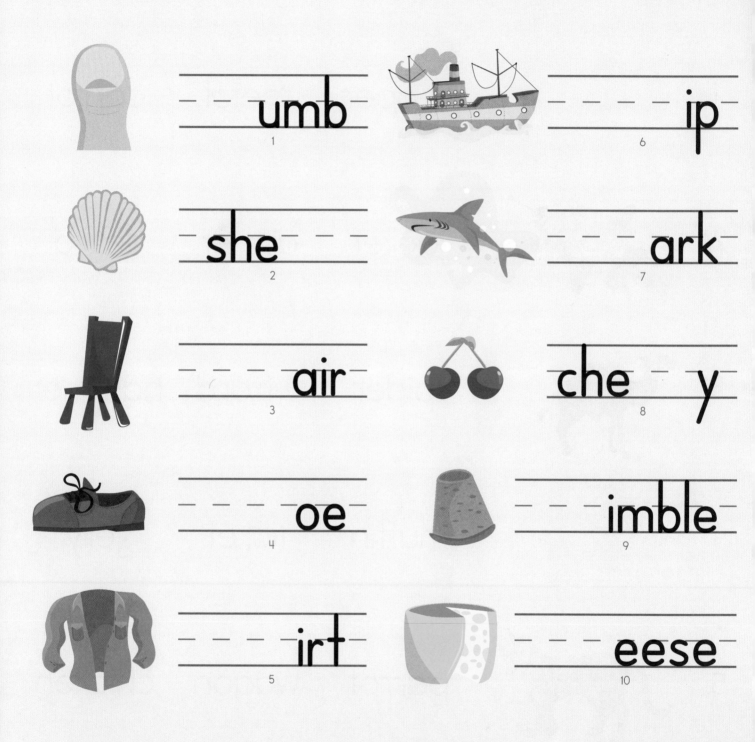

1. _____ umb
2. _____ she
3. _____ air
4. _____ oe
5. _____ irt
6. _____ ip
7. _____ ark
8. che _____ y
9. _____ imble
10. _____ eese

## Blank Out

READ each sentence and LOOK at the picture. WRITE the word to complete the sentence. LOOK at the word box for help.

| brush | beach | splash | moth | bench |
|-------|-------|--------|------|-------|

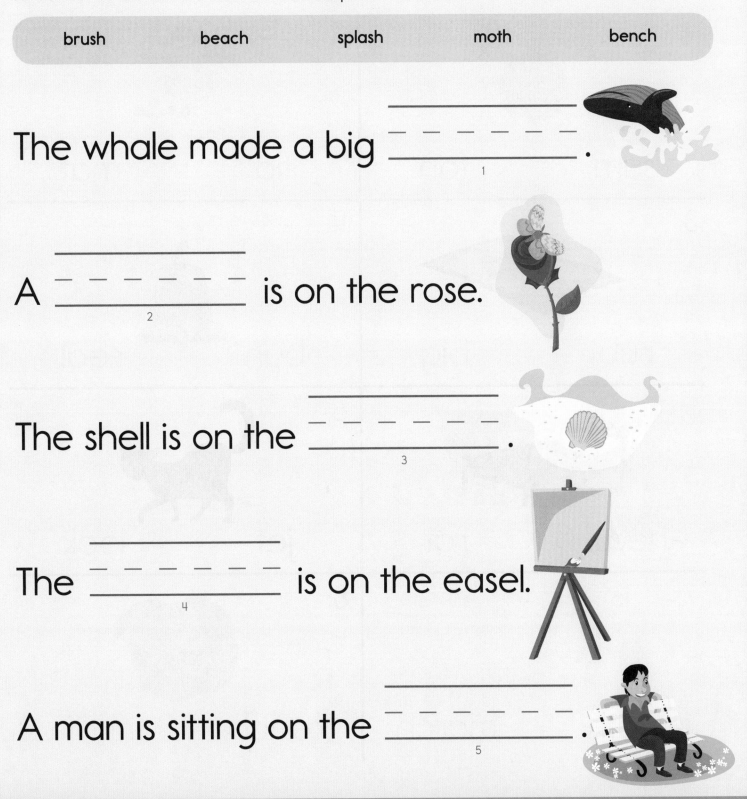

The whale made a big _____ . 1

A _____ is on the rose. 2

The shell is on the _____ . 3

The _____ is on the easel. 4

A man is sitting on the _____ . 5

# That's the End

SAY the name of each picture and LISTEN to its ending sound. CIRCLE the word that has the same ending sound.

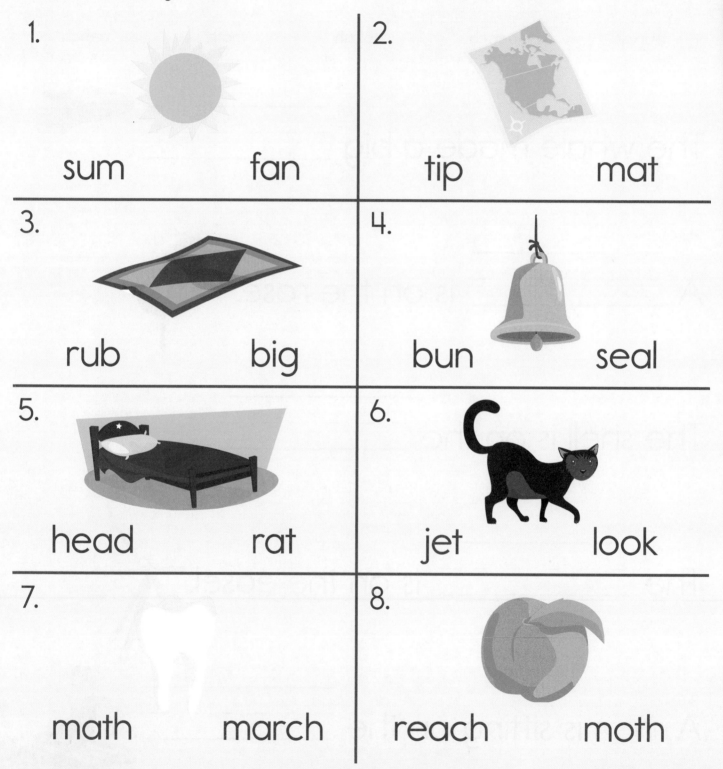

1.         sum      fan

2.         tip      mat

3.         rub      big

4.         bun      seal

5.         head      rat

6.         jet      look

7.         math      march

8.         reach      moth

## Time to Read

CIRCLE the sentence that matches the picture.

1.

The crab is in the crib.
The bug is on the rug.

2.

The kitten is on
the mitten.
The wagon is on
the muffin.

3.

The cat can jump up.
The seal rings the bell.

4.

Dad chops the wood.
I like ham and jam.

# Short Vowels

## Same Sound

The word *hat* has a short **a** in the middle.

SAY the name for each picture. WRITE "a" if you hear the short **a** sound.

# Maze Crazy!

Help the ram find the flag. DRAW a line through the maze to connect the pictures whose names have the short **a** sound.

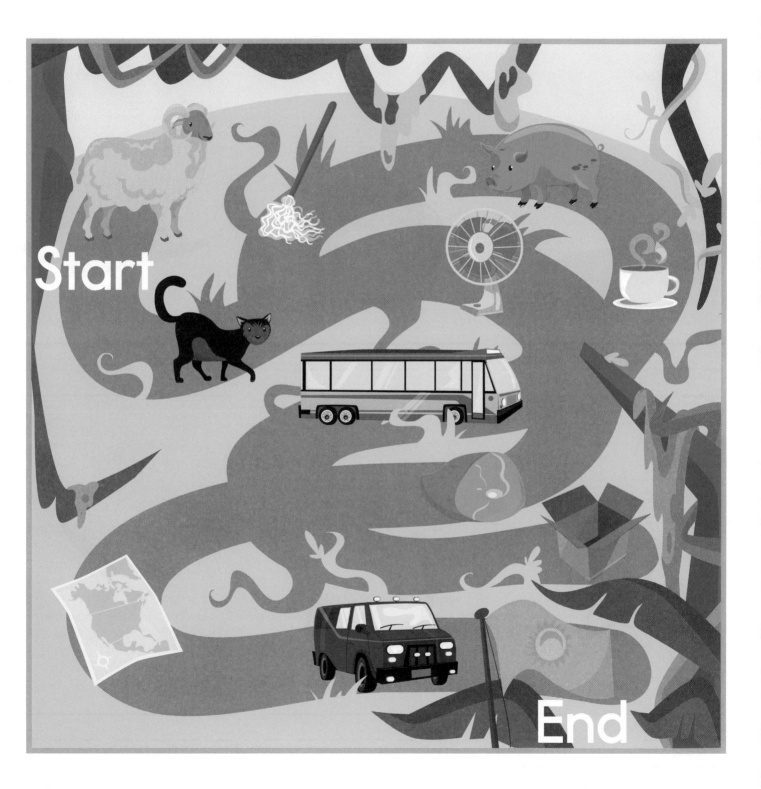

# Short Vowels

## Match and Write

The word *hen* has a short **e** in the middle.

SAY the name for each picture. FIND the correct name in the word box and CIRCLE it. Then WRITE the word.

| web | nest | pen | net | sled | bed |
|-----|------|-----|-----|------|-----|

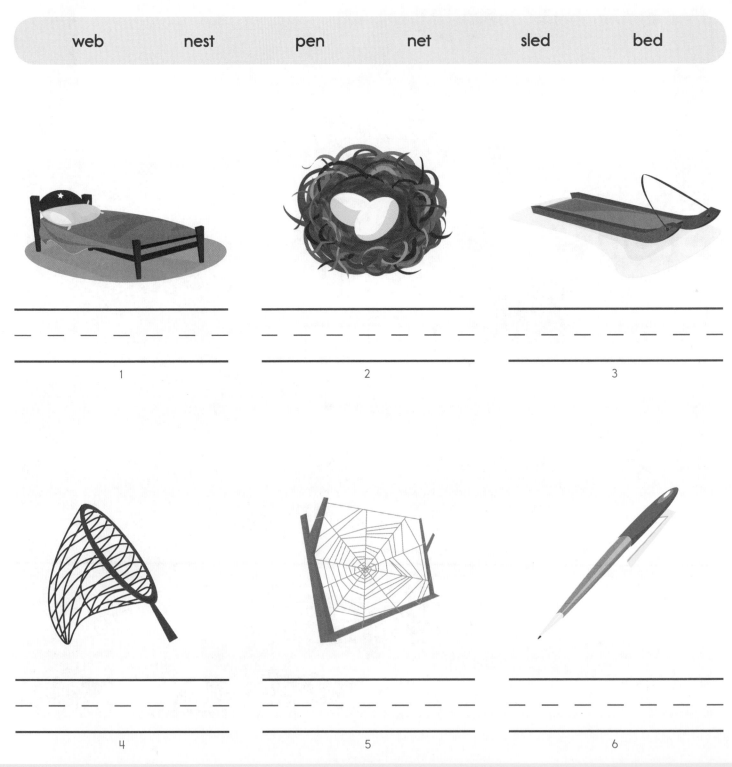

1

2

3

4

5

6

## What Am I?

WRITE the answers in the blanks. The words have the same vowel sound as in the word *hen*.

I am a bird's home.

_____
- - - - - - - - - -
_____
1

I am what a
hen lays.

_____
- - - - - - - - - -
_____
2

I am the number that
comes after nine.

**10**

_____
- - - - - - - - - -
_____
3

I am what a spider
spins.

_____
- - - - - - - - - -
_____
4

I am what you
sleep in.

_____
- - - - - - - - - -
_____
5

# Short Vowels

## Match Up

The word *wig* has a short **i** in the middle.

READ and TRACE each word. DRAW a line from the word to its matching picture.

pig

bib

fish

pin

quilt

## Time to Rhyme

SAY the name of each picture. CIRCLE the word or words that rhyme.

1.      hush      dish      wish

2.      pat      map      pit

3.      bib      sip      let

4.      big      peg      wig

5.      sit      mix      sack

# Short Vowels

## Same Sound

The word *dog* has a short **o** in the middle.

SAY the name for each picture. WRITE "o" if you hear the short **o** sound.

# Maze Crazy!

Help the frog leap to the rock. DRAW a line through the maze to connect the pictures whose names have the short **o** sound.

# Short Vowels

## Match and Write

The word *cup* has a short **u** sound in the middle.

SAY the name for each picture. FIND the correct name in the word box and CIRCLE it. Then WRITE the word.

| bus | mud | tub | plug | sun | rug |
|-----|-----|-----|------|-----|-----|

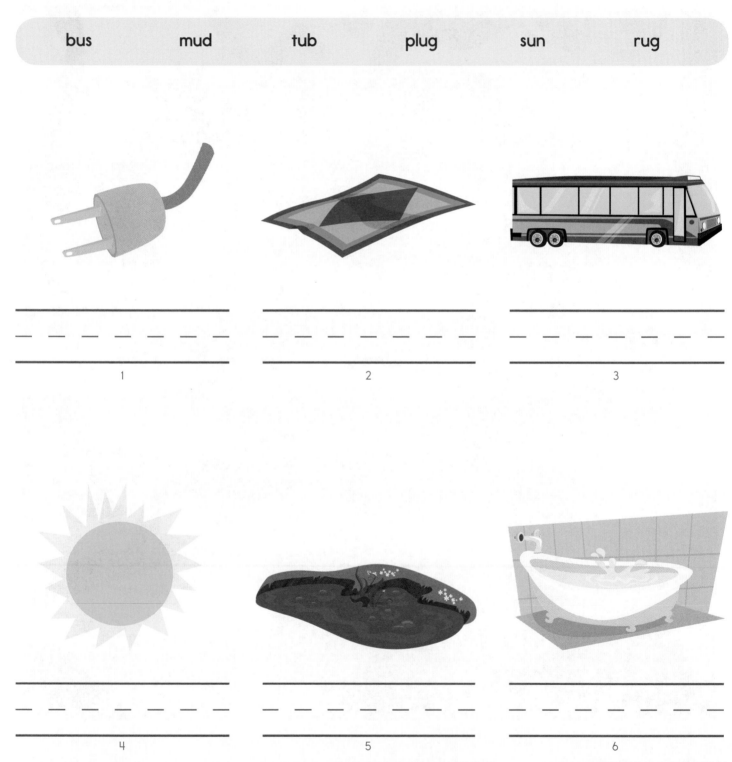

1

2

3

4

5

6

## Blank Out

READ each sentence. LOOK at the picture. WRITE the word to complete the sentence. LOOK at the word box for help.

| cup | sub | gum | rug | truck |

The bug is on the _____ .
1

The pup is as small as a _____ .
2

The _____ is in the sun.
3

It's fun to chew _____ .
4

The _____ is stuck in the mud.
5

## Same Sound

The word *vase* has a long **a** sound in the middle.

SAY the name for each picture. WRITE "a" if you hear the long **a** sound.

# Maze Crazy!

Help the snake get to the gate. DRAW a line through the maze, connecting the pictures whose names have the long **a** sound.

# Match and Write

**3**

The word *three* has a long **e** sound at the end.

SAY the name of the picture. FIND the correct name in the word box and CIRCLE it.
Then WRITE the word.

| knee | bee | sheep | green | tree | queen |

1

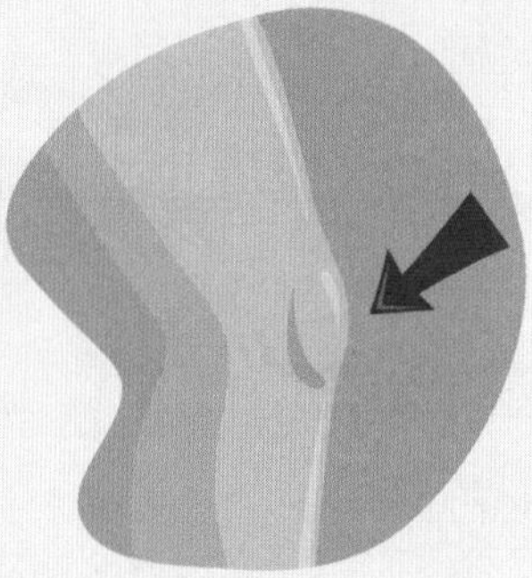

2

3

4

5

6

## What Am I?

WRITE the answers in the blanks. The words have the same vowel sound as the word *peel*.

I can make honey.

_____
_ _ _ _ _
_____
1

I am the color of trees and grass.

_____
_ _ _ _ _
_____
2

I can go around and around.

_____
_ _ _ _ _
_____
3

I come after two and before four.

_____
_ _ _ _ _
_____
4

I am part of a shoe.

_____
_ _ _ _ _
_____
5

## Match Up

The word *mice* has a long **i** sound in the middle.

READ and TRACE each word. DRAW a line from the word to its matching picture.

kite

nine

slide

tie

bike

# Time to Rhyme

SAY the name of each picture. CIRCLE the word or words that rhyme.

1.       bite     cube     rope

2.       hive     save     keep

3.       pole     pave     tie

4.       wipe     ripe     dive

5.       cone     fine     dine

## Same Sound

The word *rose* has a long **o** in the middle.

SAY the name for each picture. WRITE "o" if you hear the long **o** sound.

# Maze Crazy!

Help the goat get to the boat. DRAW a line through the maze to connect the pictures whose names have the long **o** sound.

# Long Vowels

## Match and Write

Hear the long **u** sound in the word *tune*.

SAY the name of the picture. FIND the picture name in the word box and CIRCLE it. Then WRITE the word.

| flute | blue | mule | glue | tube | cube |
|-------|------|------|------|------|------|

1

2

3

4

5

6

# Blank Out

READ each sentence and LOOK at the picture. WRITE the word to complete the sentence. LOOK at the word box for help.

| mule | flute | blue | glue | cube |
|------|-------|------|------|------|

1. A _____ swam in the pool.

2. The spoon is by the _____ .

3. The goose can play the _____ .

4. The _____ is on the stool.

5. Luke has a _____ tuba.

## Same Sound

The letter "y" can have two sounds: a long **i** sound as in *cry* or a long **e** sound as in *baby*.

SAY the name for each picture. WRITE "i" if you hear the long **i** sound and "e" if you hear the long **e** sound.

---

## What Am I?

WRITE the answers in the blanks. The words have the long **i** or long **e** sound.

I sometimes do this in a pan.

_____

1

I am the month after June.

_____

2

2010

| S | M | T | W | T | F | S |
|---|---|---|---|---|---|---|
|   |   |   |   |   |   | 1 |
| 2 | 3 | 4 | 5 | 6 | 7 | 8 |
| 9 | 10 | 11 | 12 | 13 | 14 | 15 |
| 16 | 11 | 18 | 19 | 20 | 21 | 22 |
| 23 | 18 | 25 | 26 | 27 | 28 | 29 |
| 30 | 25 |   |   |   |   |   |

I am made up of many buildings.

_____

3

I sometimes take your teeth.

_____

4

I am round and red and grow.

_____

5

## Hide and Seek

READ the words in the word box. LOOK for the matching objects in the picture. CIRCLE the words that have a short vowel sound. CROSS OUT the words that have a long vowel sound.

| slide | kid | flag | rock | bee | truck | skates |
|-------|-----|------|------|-----|-------|--------|
| man | pond | pole | nest | duck | flute | kite |

## Time to Read

CIRCLE the sentence that matches the picture.

1.

The bell is in the nest.
The hen is on the egg.

2.

The frog is on the log.
The frog is in the pond.

3.

A toad is in the boat.
A goat is in the road.

4.

A cube is on a mule.
A tube is on a cube.

# Compound Words

## It Takes Two

A COMPOUND word is made of two words. The two words are put together to make a new word.

WRITE the compound word made from each pair of pictures.

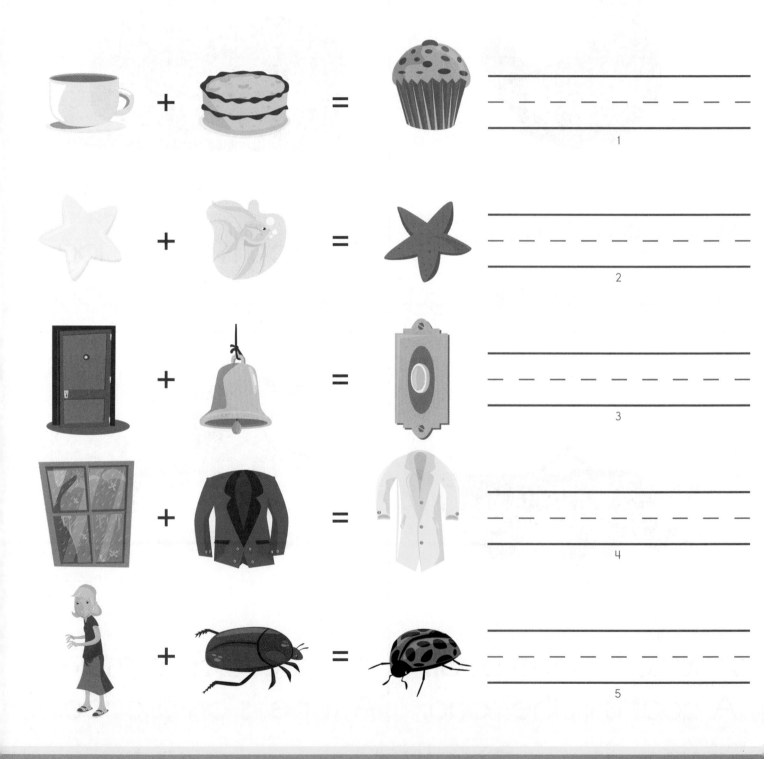

# One Plus One Makes Two

LOOK at the pictures. READ the words in the word box. WRITE the compound word that matches each pair of pictures.

| football | doghouse | snowman | rainbow | catfish |
|----------|----------|---------|---------|---------|

+ = _____
1

+ = _____
2

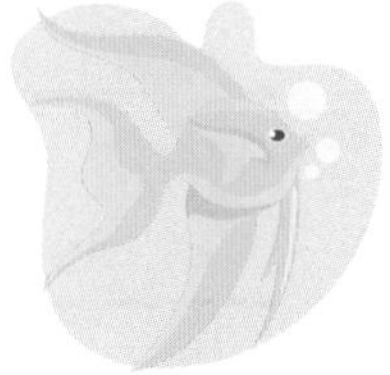

+ = _____
3

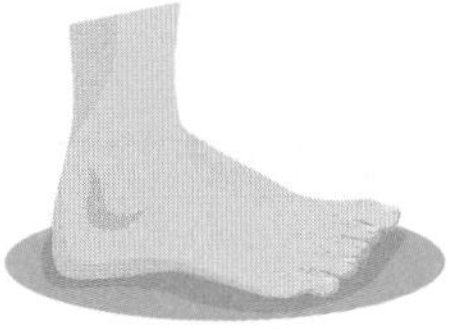

+ = _____
4

+ = _____
5

# Compound Words

## Put It Together

DRAW a line between the two words in each column that make a compound word. WRITE the compound word.

sail        shell

_ _ _ _ _ _ _ _ _ _ _ _
1

bed         cake

_ _ _ _ _ _ _ _ _ _ _ _
2

pan         box

_ _ _ _ _ _ _ _ _ _ _ _
3

sand        boat

_ _ _ _ _ _ _ _ _ _ _ _
4

sea         room

_ _ _ _ _ _ _ _ _ _ _ _
5

pea         ship

_ _ _ _ _ _ _ _ _ _ _ _
6

space       nut

_ _ _ _ _ _ _ _ _ _ _ _
7

## Word Pairs

CIRCLE the compound word in each sentence. WRITE the compound word and the two smaller words that it came from.

1. Kim and I played in the backyard.

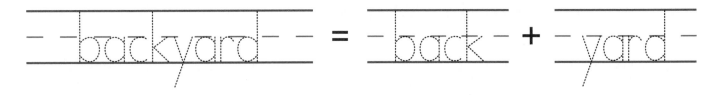

backyard = back + yard

2. My brother likes to play baseball.

_____ = _____ + _____

3. A butterfly is on the flower.

_____ = _____ + _____

4. Kate's books are in her backpack.

_____ = _____ + _____

5. Three goldfish are in the tank.

_____ = _____ + _____

## Contraction Action

### One Plus One Makes...One?

A **contraction** is a shortened form of two words. A symbol called an *apostrophe* takes the place of the missing letter or letters.

*Examples: is + not = isn't     he + is = he's*

READ the sentences. CIRCLE the contraction in each sentence. WRITE the two words that make up each contraction. LOOK at the word box for help.

| it is | I will | I am | we are | were not |
|-------|--------|------|--------|----------|

1. I'll help make the bed.

_____
_ _ _ _ _ _ _ _
_____

2. I am happy that we're going to the park.

_____
_ _ _ _ _ _ _ _
_____

3. Do you think it's going to rain today?

_____
_ _ _ _ _ _ _ _
_____

4. The birds weren't in the nest.

_____
_ _ _ _ _ _ _ _
_____

5. I'm in the first grade.

_____
_ _ _ _ _ _ _ _
_____

## It's a Match

DRAW a line from each contraction to the words it came from.

| | |
|---|---|
| I'll | were not |
| won't | you will |
| I'm | I will |
| it's | will not |
| weren't | it is |
| you'll | cannot |
| they're | do not |
| don't | they are |
| can't | I am |

## Double the Fun

When a word has two syllables with **double** consonants in the middle, such as *rabbit*, divide the word between the consonants: *rab | bit*.

DIVIDE the words into syllables. Then WRITE the syllables next to the words.

1. din|ner      _din_      _ner_

2. kitten

3. mitten

4. happen

5. puppet

6. zipper

7. muffin

8. button

# Put It Together

LOOK at each picture and the syllable next to it. FILL IN the rest of each word with a syllable from the word box.

| low | za | ten | mer | ple | py |
|-----|----|----|----|----|----|

1. ap _ple_

2. ham _____

3. mit _____

4. piz _____

5. pup _____

6. yel _____

# Syllables

## Split It Up

When a word has two syllables with **any two consonants** in the middle, you can usually divide the word between the consonants.

DIVIDE the words into syllables. Then WRITE the syllables next to the words.

1. nap|kin          nap          kin

2. basket

3. doctor

4. picnic

5. monkey

6. winter

7. sister

8. pencil

# Put It Together

SAY the name for each animal. FILL IN the rest of each word with a syllable from the word box.

| pen | wal | mon | tur | tur | roos |
|-----|-----|-----|-----|-----|------|

1.  _____ rus

2.  _____ key

3.  _____ tle

4.  _____ ter

5.  _____ key

6.  _____ guin

# Plurals

## More than One

A word is **singular** when it names one person, place, or thing. A word is **plural** when it names more than one person, place, or thing. An "-s" at the end of a word often means there is more than one.

LOOK at each picture. CIRCLE the word that means the same thing as the picture. WRITE the word.

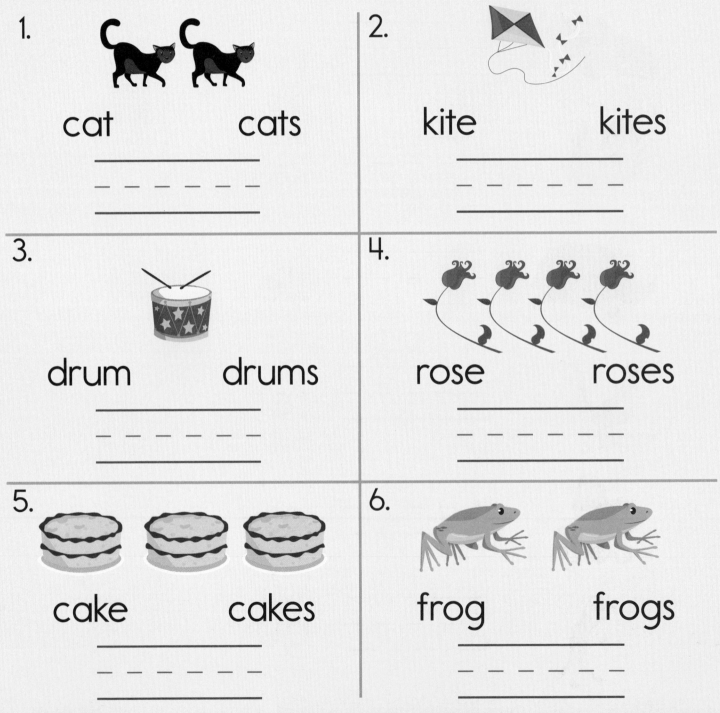

1.    cat    cats

2.    kite    kites

3.    drum    drums

4.    rose    roses

5.    cake    cakes

6.    frog    frogs

## Make It More

READ each sentence. LOOK at the underlined word in the sentence. WRITE the plural of the word on the line.

1. They gave her a <u>gift</u>. _____

2. That <u>map</u> is old. _____

3. Kim is flying a <u>kite</u>. _____

4. I read that <u>book</u>. _____

5. The <u>cup</u> is in the sink. _____

6. The <u>dog</u> is barking. _____

7. I see a <u>bird</u> in the nest. _____

8. My aunt baked a <u>cake</u>. _____

## Alternate Endings

Add "-s" to make most words plural. Add "-es" if the word ends in "sh," "ch," "tch," "s," or "x."

LOOK at the pictures. TRACE the words. ADD "-s" or "-es" to make the words plural.

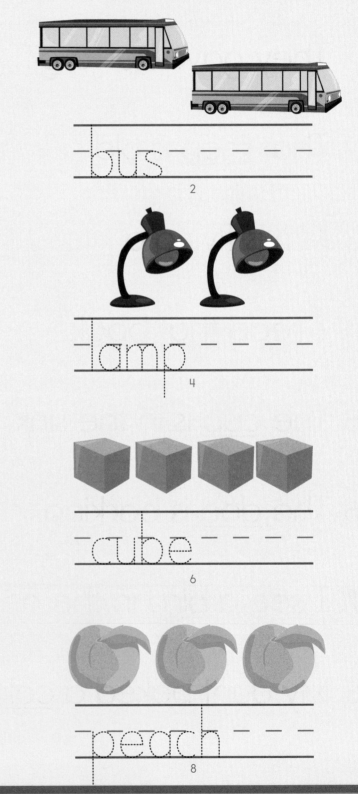

dress
1

bus
2

brush
3

lamp
4

bike
5

cube
6

box
7

peach
8

## Alternate Endings

Usually, when a word ends in "f," we change it to "v" and add "-es" to make the word plural.

LOOK at each picture. CIRCLE the word that means the same thing as the picture. WRITE the word.

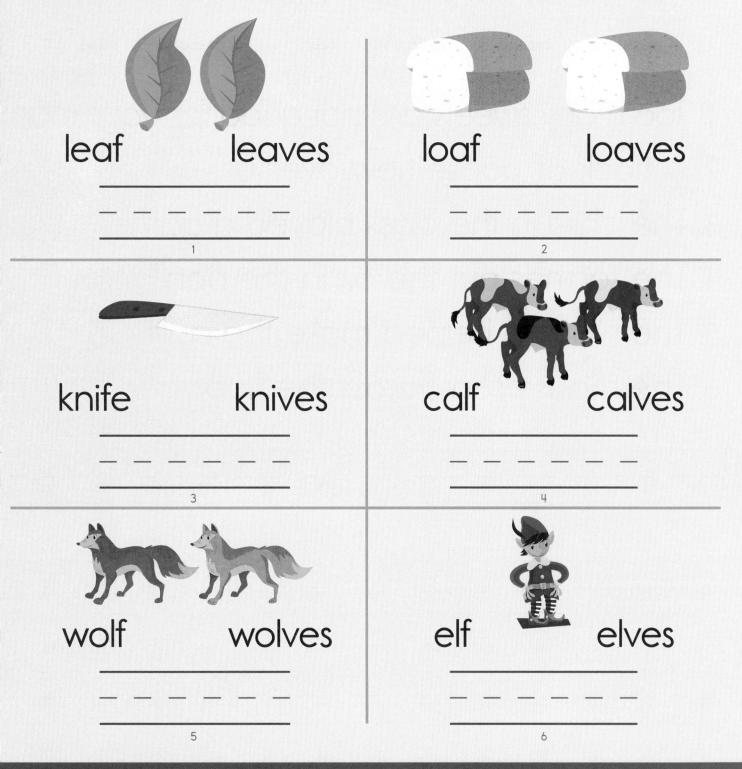

leaf    leaves

1

loaf    loaves

2

knife    knives

3

calf    calves

4

wolf    wolves

5

elf    elves

6

## More Ways than One

Not all plurals end in "-s" or "-es." For example, the plural of *foot* is *feet*.

READ each sentence and CHANGE the word in **purple** to plural. WRITE the plural words on the numbered lines. USE the words in the word box.

| women | oxen | children | teeth | geese | mice |

1. Too many sweets are not good for your tooth

2. A flock of goose flew over us.

3. The child in the class played a game.

4. The farmer put the ox in the pen.

5. The woman helped make the quilt.

6. The mouse ran across the floor.

_____           _____
_ _ _ _ _ _ _ _ _ _ _ _ _           _ _ _ _ _ _ _ _ _ _ _ _ _
_____           _____
            1                                   2

_____           _____
_ _ _ _ _ _ _ _ _ _ _ _ _           _ _ _ _ _ _ _ _ _ _ _ _ _
_____           _____
            3                                   4

_____           _____
_ _ _ _ _ _ _ _ _ _ _ _ _           _ _ _ _ _ _ _ _ _ _ _ _ _
_____           _____
            5                                   6

# More Ways than One

MAKE these words plural.

foot

_____
1

goose

_____
4

tooth

_____
2

man

_____
5

child

_____
3

MAKE these words singular.

oxen

_____
6

mice

_____
9

firemen

_____
7

women

_____
10

people

_____
8

# Put It Together

LOOK at the two pictures. SAY each picture name and then SAY them together.
CIRCLE the word that makes the compound word.

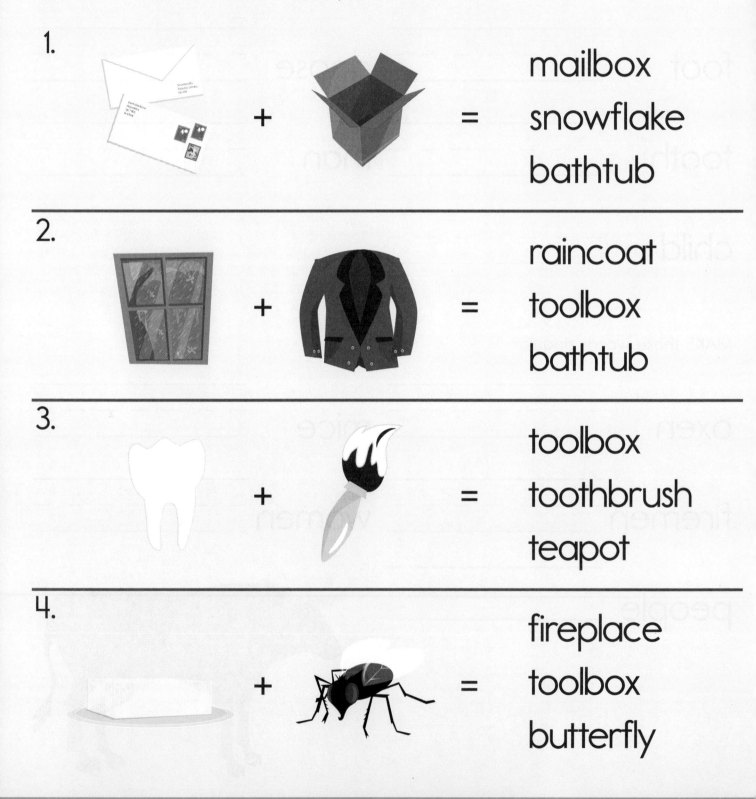

1.
+ =
mailbox
snowflake
bathtub

2.
+ =
raincoat
toolbox
bathtub

3.
+ =
toolbox
toothbrush
teapot

4.
+ =
fireplace
toolbox
butterfly

## Match Up

MATCH the words on the left to the correct contraction.

I will                   we're

it is                   you're

they are            I'll

we are               they're

you are             it's

## More Ways than One

WRITE the plural for each word.

cat            _____ 1      leaf      _____ 6

rose          _____ 2      peach    _____ 7

dress       _____ 3      knife     _____ 8

woman    _____ 4      mouse    _____ 9

ox             _____ 5      foot      _____ 10

# Words to Know

## Word Blocks

FIND the word from the word box that completes each sentence. WRITE it in the blocks.
USE each word only once.

| old | just | four | round | sleep | fly |

1. The sun and an orange are r o u n d .

2. You are [____] as tall as I am.

3. Can you see the [____] birds in the tree?

4. A jet can [____] fast.

5. My grandpa is very [____] .

6. The baby will [____] in her crib.

## Riddle Me This

READ each riddle. CHOOSE a word from the word box to solve the riddle. WRITE it next to each riddle.

| old | just | four | round | sleep | fly |
|-----|------|------|-------|-------|-----|

1. I am what a bird can do.  _____

2. I come after three and before five.  _____

3. I am the opposite of young.  _____

4. I am what you do when you are in bed.  _____

5. I am the shape of a ball.  _____

6. I rhyme with the word *must*.  _____

## Words to Know

### Match Up

READ each phrase and then MATCH it to the correct picture.

1. very old

2. went to sleep

3. just think

4. four of them

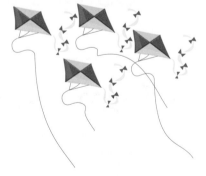

5. is round

6. can fly

## The Right Word

READ the words under each sentence. USE one of the words to complete the sentence.

1. Did you see the bee _____ to its hive?

| ask | fly | think |

2. I ate _____ carrots with dinner.

| four | sleep | after |

3. A tire and a circle are _____ .

| some | every | round |

4. Mom said, "Please take _____ one."

| just | with | again |

5. That _____ woman is my great aunt.

| just | right | old |

## Word Blocks

FIND the word from the word box that completes each sentence. WRITE it in the blocks. USE each word only once.

| over | stop | give | sing | open | green |
|------|------|------|------|------|-------|

1. I love to hear the birds ____.

2. Peas and limes are ____.

3. It's fun to ____ gifts.

4. The plane flew ____ the lake.

5. We sat on the bench at the bus ____.

6. I will ____ you half of the money.

## Riddle Me This

READ each riddle. CHOOSE a word from the word box to solve the riddle. WRITE it next to each riddle.

| over | stop | give | open | green |
|------|------|------|------|-------|

1. I am the color of grass and trees.

         _____

2. I am the opposite of *closed.*

         _____

3. I rhyme with the word *clover.*

         _____

4. I am what you do at a red light.

         _____

5. I am the opposite of *take.*

         _____

## Match Up

READ each phrase and then MATCH it to the correct picture.

1. they can sing

2. please stop

3. over there

4. will give

5. it is green

6. is open

## The Right Word

READ the words under each sentence. USE one of the words to complete the sentence.

1. You should _____ and look both ways before you cross the street.

| know | take | stop |

2. I will _____ you a gift for your birthday.

| like | give | write |

3. The dog pushed the door _____ .

| open | what | after |

4. I love to hear the children _____ that song.

| sing | put | take |

5. Blue and yellow make _____ .

| some | round | green |

## Stack Up

LOOK at the words and pictures. WRITE the names of the pictures in the correct columns.

lemon

corn

apple

carrot

orange

grapes

broccoli

lettuce

# Fruits

_____

- - - - - - - - - - - - -

_____

_____

_____

_____

_____

# Vegetables

_____

- - - - - - - - - - - - -

_____

_____

_____

_____

_____

# Odd Word Out

CIRCLE the picture in each row that does **not** go with the others.

1.

cookies · cupcake · olive · pie

2.

ladybug · butterfly · dog · bee

3.

yarn · pants · dress · shirt

WRITE the names of the pictures that do **not** belong.

1

2

3

## Stack Up

LOOK at the words and pictures. WRITE the names of the pictures in the correct columns.

shorts

sandals

earmuffs

swimsuit

scarf

mittens

# Summer Clothes

_____

- - - - - - - - - - - - -

_____

- - - - - - - - - - - - -

_____

- - - - - - - - - - - - -

_____

- - - - - - - - - - - - -

# Winter Clothes

_____

- - - - - - - - - - - - -

_____

- - - - - - - - - - - - -

_____

- - - - - - - - - - - - -

_____

- - - - - - - - - - - - -

## Odd Word Out

CIRCLE the picture in each row that does **not** go with the others.

1.

five       green       yellow       blue

2.

goat       cow       tiger       pig

3.

bat       rake       hoe       shovel

WRITE the names of the pictures that do **not** belong.

_____       _____

1       2

_____

3

# Words That Go Together

## Stack Up

LOOK at the words and pictures. WRITE the names of the pictures in the correct columns.

daisy

pine

oak

rose

tulip

palm

willow

pansy

## Flowers

_____

- - - - - - - - - - - - - -

_____

- - - - - - - - - - - - - -

_____

- - - - - - - - - - - - - -

_____

- - - - - - - - - - - - - -

_____

## Trees

_____

- - - - - - - - - - - - - -

_____

- - - - - - - - - - - - - -

_____

- - - - - - - - - - - - - -

_____

- - - - - - - - - - - - - -

_____

# Odd Word Out

CIRCLE the picture in each row that does **not** go with the others.

1.

rooster          owl          balloon          penguin

2.

knife          key          fork          spoon

3.

kite          basketball          soccer ball          baseball

WRITE the names of the pictures that do **not** belong.

1

2

3

## Blank Out

READ the story. USE the words in the word box to finish the story.

| over | open | fly | green | stop | old | just | sing |

One day Tess went for a walk. She saw an

_____ (1) man. The old man said, "Please

_____ (2) !" He asked Tess to _____ (3)

a song. She sang for _____ (4) a few

minutes. When the song was _____ (5) ,

the old man gave her a _____ (6) box to

_____ (7) . He said, "Make a wish." Tess

wished that she could _____ (8) . And

then she flew away!

# Name It

LOOK at each group of pictures. THINK about how they go together. CHECK the correct name for each group.

1.

☐ Things you find in the kitchen

☐ Things you find at the beach

☐ Things you find in a bedroom

2.

☐ Things that are eaten

☐ Things that are tools

☐ Things that are toys

3.

☐ Things that are zoo animals

☐ Things that are insects

☐ Things that are green

4.

☐ Things that live in ponds

☐ Things that have fur

☐ Things that can hop

# The Big Idea

## It's All in the Picture

The **main idea** is the most important idea in a story. It's the big idea. It tells what the story is about.

READ the stories and CIRCLE the picture that best tells the story's main idea.

> ### Best Friends
> Marta and Nicky are best friends. They walk to school together. They ride bikes together. They read books together. They play ball together. Marta and Nicky do everything together.

## See and Hear Farm Animals

You can see and hear many animals on a farm. You can see horses. Horses neigh. You can see cows. Cows moo. You can see pigs. Pigs oink. What other animals can you see and hear on a farm?

# The Big Idea

## Name It

READ the stories. CHECK the box next to the best title for each story.

Trees are homes for many animals. Squirrels live in trees. They hide nuts in the trees.

Bees live in trees. They make hives in the trees.

Birds live in trees. They build nests in the trees. Many animals live in trees.

☐ Bees and Hives

☐ Trees Are Homes

☐ Birds Make Nests

Rosa is a baker. One of the best cakes she ever made was for a man named Mr. Lee. He wanted a special cake for his wife's birthday party. Mrs. Lee loves cats. So Rosa made her a cake with cats on it.

Mrs. Lee thought the cake was the best cake she had ever seen. She did not want to cut it. Mr. Lee said that their guests were waiting to eat cake. Mrs. Lee almost cried when she had to cut the cake. But she loved the way it tasted.

☐ A Special Cake

☐ Cats Are Special

☐ A Birthday Party

# The Big Idea

## What's the Big Idea?

READ the stories. CHECK the sentence that tells the main idea.

### Wishes

Have you ever wished for something? My little sister wishes for a new doll and new shoes. My big brother wishes for a computer and a car. I wish that I could fly and travel to the moon. What do you wish for?

☐ People make wishes.

☐ Wishing to fly is better than wishing for a new doll.

☐ You should be happy with what you have.

### Buster

Buster likes to do a lot of things. He likes to fetch his rubber ball. He likes to chase butterflies and dig holes. He likes to have his tummy rubbed and his back scratched. But most of all, Buster loves to go for walks in the park.

☐ Buster can fetch a ball.

☐ Buster likes to do many things.

☐ Buster loves to go for walks.

## Details, Details

Details tell about the main idea. They can tell who, what, where, when, and how. READ the story. CIRCLE the pictures that show details from the story.

### Different but the Same

Lily and Nate are both different and the same. They are different because Lily is tall and Nate is short. Lily plays soccer and Nate plays baseball. Lily has a cat and Nate has a dog. Lily lives in an apartment and Nate lives in a house.

Lily and Nate are the same because Lily likes Nate just the way he is. And Nate likes Lily just the way she is. Lily and Nate say, "That's how friends are."

# Who?

# What?

# Where?

## Details, Details

READ the story.

### Careful Grace

It was a cold, snowy winter day. Papa and Grace drove a car to the park. They walked to the ice rink inside the park. Papa was going to teach Grace to ice skate.

Papa showed Grace how to put on her skates and how to walk in them. Grace held Papa's hand tightly as the two of them skated around the rink.

At last, Grace let go of Papa's hand. She began to glide on the ice. Papa waved at Grace. She waved back. She hoped that it was not time to stop.

READ each sentence. CIRCLE the picture that matches what happens in the story.

# 1. How do Papa and Grace get to the park?

# 2. What kind of day is it?

# 3. Where did Papa and Grace go?

## Yes or No?

READ the story.

### Mammals

A mammal is a certain kind of animal. Mammals have hair or fur. Mammals take good care of their babies. Mammals drink their mother's milk.

A tiger is a mammal that lives in the jungles of Asia. Its stripes help it hide in the tall grass.

A pig is a mammal that lives on a farm. It likes to eat corn and roll in the mud.

A bat is a mammal that lives in many places. It can fly.

A whale is a mammal that lives in the ocean. It must come up to breathe air.

Guess what? You are a mammal too!

READ each sentence. WRITE **true** if the sentence matches what you read in the story. WRITE **false** if it does not.

1. All mammals have feathers.

2. Pigs like to eat corn.

3. A whale does not need to breathe air.

4. Humans are mammals.

5. Tigers can hide in the tall grass.

## First, Next, Last

A story has a beginning, a middle, and an end. READ the story. What happens first? Next? Last? WRITE 1, 2, and 3 in the boxes to show the correct order.

### Time to Garden

"Time to get up!" said Mom and Dad.

"Why?" asked Kate and Tim.

"We're going to plant a garden," said Mom and Dad.

Kate and Tim got up and got dressed. Then they ate breakfast.

Mom, Dad, Kate, and Tim drove to the garden shop. They bought flower seeds and some gardening tools.

When they got home, Dad dug up the dirt. Kate and Tim poked holes in the dirt. Kate and Tim put a few seeds in each hole. Then they covered the holes with dirt. Mom watered the seeds.

"Now we just have to wait," said Dad. "The plants will grow into pretty flowers," said Mom.

Kate and Tim smiled.

☐ Mom waters the garden.

☐ Kate and Tim plant the seeds.

☐ Dad digs up the dirt.

READ the story. What happens first? Next? Last? WRITE 1, 2, and 3 in the boxes to show the correct order.

### Market Day

Today is market day. First Grandma and Juan stop by to see Mr. Sanchez the baker. The air is filled with delicious smells. Grandma buys two loaves of bread. When they leave, Mr. Sanchez hands Juan a cookie.

Their next stop is the fruit stand. They buy grapes, peaches, and plums. Grandma gets some flowers just before they leave.

At home, Grandma puts the flowers in a vase and Juan unpacks the food. Then he eats a ripe, juicy peach.

☐ Grandma and Juan stop at the baker's.

☐ Juan eats a peach.

☐ Grandma buys some flowers.

# Order of Events

## Picture Order

Sometimes stories have words like "first," "next," "after," and "last." These words give you clues about the order of events in the story.

LOOK at the pictures and READ the sentences. LOOK for the word clues. Then NUMBER the pictures from 1 to 4 to show the order in the stories.

Then Alex looks under the bed. She is not behind the door. She is not under the bed.

After Mom hides, Alex looks behind the door. She is not there.

Alex looks in the closet last. There is Mom!

Mom hides first.

Finally, Mia puts the leaves into a big bag.

Then Mia rakes the leaves into a big pile.

First, Mia gets a rake.

Next, Mia begins to rake.

## Story Order

READ the story.

### Hello, Frog!

It's time for newborn frogs! A baby frog is called a tadpole. A tadpole has a large head. Its body is round. It has a long tail. It wiggles its long tail to help it swim. The tadpole grows fast. Its body gets bigger. It grows legs. Then it loses its tail. Now it is a frog.

Now NUMBER the pictures from 1 to 4 to show the order.

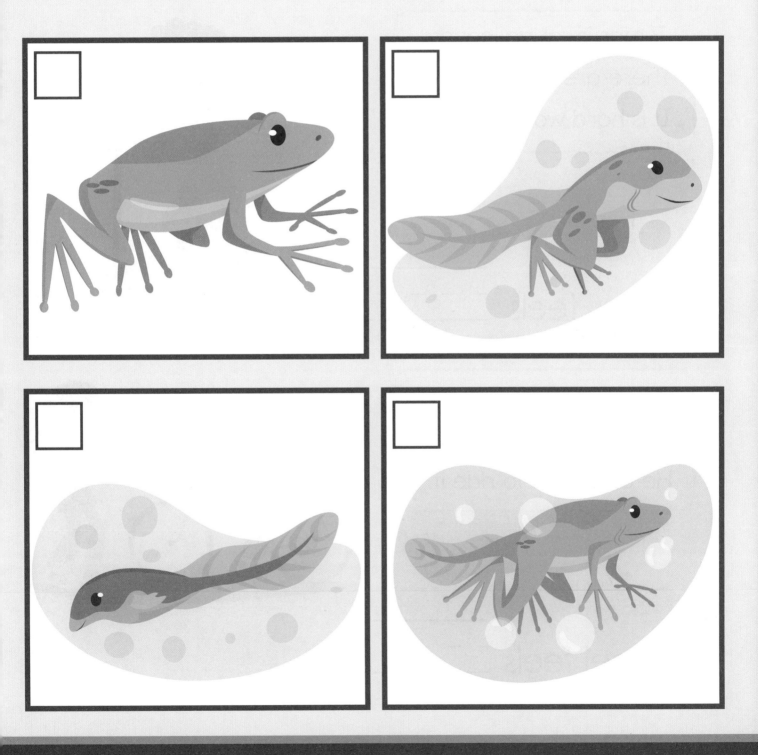

## Looking for Clues

Sometimes writers don't tell you everything in a story. You need to look for clues or "read between the lines" to think about what the writer means.

READ each story. LOOK at the picture for clues. FIND the word that best describes the person in the story to complete the sentence.

1.

> Jamar is raking leaves.
>
> There are a lot of leaves.
>
> It is hard work.

tired          upset

Jamar feels _____ .

2.

> Marcel got a new bike.
>
> It is big and blue.
>
> He can't wait to ride it.

silly          excited

Marcel feels _____ .

3. Annie lost her ring.

She has looked everywhere for it.

Where could it be?

lucky          sad

Annie feels _____.

4. Annie found her ring.
It was under her bed.

She puts the ring on her finger.

sleepy          happy

Annie feels _____.

## Looking for Clues

READ each part of the story. THINK about what the writer is saying. Then CIRCLE the correct answer.

### Beach Vacation

Jason and Jenna are going to camp at the beach. They help Mom and Dad get ready for the trip. They have to buy food. They have to pack the gear. They have to load the van.

1. Getting ready for a camping trip can be _____.

   a. a lot of work

   b. a waste of time

   c. too easy

The beach is a lot of fun. Jason and Jenna play in the sand. They search for shells. They dig for clams. They swim in the water. They help make the meals. Usually they just have cereal for breakfast and sandwiches for lunch. But for dinner, they fix something special.

Jason and Jenna like roasting hot dogs over the fire. Then it is time for bed.

2. What is it like to camp at the beach?
   a. boring
   b. busy
   c. scary

## Looking for Clues

READ each part of the story. THINK about what the writer is saying. Then CIRCLE the correct answer.

### Sparrow Finds a Friend

Sparrow had a problem. All the other birds were bigger than he was. Sparrow decided to look for other birds his size. He met Crow. But Crow was much bigger than he was.

He met Woodpecker. But Woodpecker was also much bigger than he was. Sparrow kept looking until he was too tired to fly any more. He rested.

A large plump bird waddled up to Sparrow.

1. What can you tell about Sparrow in this part of the story?
   a. He thinks a friend should be his size.
   b. He does not like Crow or Woodpecker.
   c. He wishes he were not a sparrow.

READ the next part of the story.

"Hello," she said, "I am Duck. You are a beautiful bird."

"No, I'm not. I am too small," said Sparrow.

"Your size makes you special," replied Duck. "Would you like to be my friend?"

"But we are not the same size," Sparrow said. "How can we be friends?"

Duck said, "We're both birds, aren't we? It doesn't matter that we are different."

The two birds flew off. Sparrow had found a new friend.

2. What can you tell about sparrow in this part of the story?
   a. He thinks Duck is a beautiful bird.
   b. He thinks it is better to be big.
   c. He wishes that Duck would go away.

## Pick the One

Sometimes you can tell or *predict* what a book is about by looking at the picture on the cover.

LOOK at the picture on each cover. CIRCLE the title that best shows what the story might be about.

1.

a. *Time to Garden*

b. *Learn to Skate*

c. *Leaves Are Changing*

2.

a. *Many Animals Live in Ponds*

b. *Ducks and Other Birds*

c. *Frog and Turtle Are Friends*

3.

a. *Water Play*

b. *Dog Wash*

c. *Time to Swim*

## And Then . . .

READ the beginning of the story. Then PREDICT what will happen next. UNDERLINE the correct answer.

---

### Sam's Vacation

Sam is going to stay with his uncle and aunt for the summer. They live on a farm.

Sam's mother grew up on a farm. She told Sam stories about how much fun she had on the farm. Sam was excited. But he worried about being away from home all summer. "There is so much to do," said Sam's mother. "You'll love it."

Sam was surprised when he first saw the farm. It looked so different from where he lived. He was used to seeing many cars and big buildings. Here he saw only a white house and a red barn.

The next morning, Sam woke up early. His uncle showed him how to milk a cow. After lunch, he learned how to feed the chickens and pigs.

After dinner, Sam got a phone call. It was his mother. She asked, "Did you enjoy your day?"

"I sure did," Sam said excitedly. "I can't wait for tomorrow."

---

## What do you think Sam will do tomorrow?

a. Milk the cow and feed the chickens and pigs

b. Ask to go home

c. Stay inside all day

## Detective Work

READ the story and LOOK for clues. PREDICT what will happen next. WRITE your prediction on the blank line.

### Rosie's Problem

Rosie shook the coins out of her piggy bank. She had been saving for a long time. She counted the coins. She had saved ten dollars. But Rosie had a big problem. She did not know what to buy with her money. She asked her mom. She asked her dad. She even asked her little brother. No one had an answer. Mom said, "Why don't we go to the toy store?"

There were so many toys. Rosie looked at the toy cars. She looked at the dolls. She looked at the games. Rosie was sad. She did not know how to spend her money. "Let's just go home, Mom," Rosie sighed.

Someone was holding a box of puppies in front of the toy store. Rosie stopped and read the sign on the box. A big smile spread across her face. She knew exactly what to do.

## How do you think Rosie most likely spent her money?

Rosie most likely spent her money on

_____

_____

## Fact or Opinion?

A **fact** is something that is true or can be proven. An **opinion** is something that is somebody's own idea.

READ the sentences. DECIDE if each sentence is a fact or an opinion. Then WRITE the sentences in the correct columns.

Orange juice tastes good.

There are seven days in a week.

Earth has only one moon.

Blue is the prettiest color.

Dogs are the best pets ever.

Roses come in many colors.

Fact

Opinion

## Fact or Opinion?

READ the story. Then READ the sentences on the next page. WRITE **F** if the sentence is a fact. WRITE **O** if the sentence is somebody's opinion.

### A Funny Bird

Penguins are interesting birds. Penguins cannot fly. But they can swim fast. They are shaped like a bullet. This helps them swim. They use their wings to move themselves through the water.

Penguins cannot breathe underwater. But they can hold their breath for a long time.

The only time penguins are in the air is when they leap out of the water to get on land. They also jump high into the air to get a gulp of air before diving back down for fish. They look funny when they do this. Penguins are interesting animals.

1. Penguins are interesting birds. _____

2. Penguins cannot fly. _____

3. They use their wings to move themselves through the water. _____

4. Penguins cannot breathe underwater. _____

5. They look funny when they do this. _____

## Details, Details

READ the story. Then ANSWER the questions on the next page.

Yoli woke up early. "What day is it?" asked Yoli.

"Saturday," said Mom.

"Yippee!" yelled Yoli. "It's time to go shopping."

Yoli went to a yard sale first. "Yoo-hoo! Do you have any yarn for sale?" she asked.

"Yes, I have yarn for sale," said a man.

"Yippie!" yelled Yoli. She put the yarn inside her bag.

Yoli went to the toy store next. "Yoo-hoo! Do you have any yo-yos for sale?" she asked.

"Yes, I have yo-yos for sale," said the clerk.

"Yippie!" yelled Yoli. She put a yo-yo inside her bag.

Then Yoli went to the grocery store. "Yoo-hoo! Do you have any yams for sale?" she asked.

"Yes, I have yams for sale," said the grocer.

"Yippie!" yelled Yoli. She put a yam inside her bag.

Yoli went to the bakery last. "Yoo-hoo! Do you have any yellow cupcakes for sale?" she asked.

"Yes, I have yellow cupcakes for sale," said the baker.

"Yippie!" yelled Yoli. She put a yellow cupcake inside her bag. Yoli said, "I am hungry." So she went home to lunch.

CIRCLE the best name for this story. Think about the main idea of the story.

Yoli Goes Shopping          The Yard Sale          Yarn and Yams

CIRCLE the correct details from the story.

1. What does Yoli buy at the toy store?
   a. a kite  b. a ball  c. a yo-yo

2. Who sells yams?
   a. the baker  b. the grocer  c. the toy clerk

3. What color is the cupcake?
   a. yellow  b. pink  c. green

4. When does Yoli go shopping?
   a. in the morning  b. at noon  c. at night

WRITE a number in each box to show the order of the story.

**Page 2**
1. bike
2. bed
3. fish
4. goat
5. dog
6. desk
7. bus
8. fork
9. doll
10. gum

**Page 3**

**Page 4**
1. quick, quit
2. jeans, jam
3. kite, kick
4. hand
5. keep

**Page 5**
1. hand
2. king
3. queen
4. jar
5. kite
6. quilt
7. hat
8. jug

**Page 6**
**l:** leaf, log
**m:** mat, mop
**n:** nose, net
**p:** pan, pig

**Page 7**

**Page 8**
1. tent
2. ring
3. tooth
4. rooster
5. tomato
6. seal
7. six
8. red
9. tub
10. saw

**Page 9**

rake — sun
rose — tape
tooth — sink
top — rock
tie — sock
rug — seal

**Page 10**
**v:** van, vase
**w:** wig, web
**y:** yellow, yo-yo
**z:** zipper, zebra

**Page 11**

v  es  wi
an  vt  ng
x-  ay  rn  ze
r  ya  ro

1. van
2. vest
3. wing
4. x-ray
5. yarn
6. zero

**Page 12**
1. kid, cage
2. cent, sip
3. get, give
4. jump, gem

**Page 13**

**Page 14**

**Page 15**
1. The cat is on the bed.
2. The pig is in the mud.
3. The queen eats ham.
4. The zebra wears a wig.

**Page 16**
1. red
2. sub
3. mop
4. drum
5. fan
6. hand
7. crib
8. ram
9. top
10. moon

**Page 17**
1. gum, clam
2. moon
3. food, sad
4. jump, top
5. rub

**Page 18**

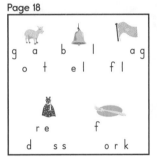

g  a  b  l  a g
o  t  e l  f l
r e  f
d  s  s  or k

1. goat
2. bell
3. flag
4. dress
5. fork

**Page 19**

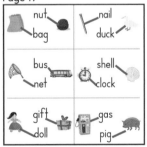

nut — bag
nail — duck
bus — net
shell — clock
gift — doll
gas — pig

**Page 20**
1. mitten
2. seven
3. pillow
4. hammer
5. zipper
6. robot
7. lemon
8. kitten
9. ladder
10. puppy

**Page 21**
1. metal
2. jacket
3. hammer
4. jelly
5. wagon

**Page 22**
1. thumb
2. shell
3. chair
4. shoe
5. shirt
6. ship
7. shark
8. cherry
9. thimble
10. cheese

**Page 23**
1. splash
2. moth
3. beach
4. brush
5. bench

**Page 24**
1. fan
2. tip
3. big
4. seal
5. head
6. jet
7. math
8. reach

**Page 25**
1. The crab is in the crib.
2. The kitten is on the mitten.
3. The seal rings the bell.
4. Dad chops the wood.

**Page 26**

**Page 27**

# Answers

**Page 28**
1. bed
2. nest
3. sled
4. net
5. web
6. pen

**Page 29**
1. nest
2. egg
3. ten
4. web
5. bed

**Page 30**

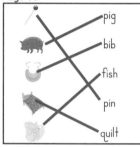

pig
bib
fish
pin
quilt

**Page 31**
1. dish, wish
2. pit
3. bib
4. big, wig
5. mix

**Page 32**

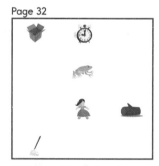

**Page 33**

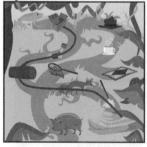

**Page 34**
1. plug
2. rug
3. bus
4. sun
5. mud
6. tub

**Page 35**
1. rug
2. cup
3. sub
4. gum
5. truck

**Page 36**

**Page 37**

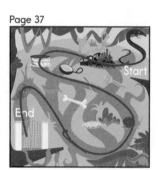

**Page 38**
1. tree
2. knee
3. queen
4. bee
5. green
6. sheep

**Page 39**
1. bee
2. green
3. wheel
4. three
5. heel

**Page 40**

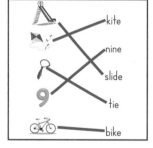

kite
nine
slide
tie
bike

**Page 41**
1. bite
2. hive
3. tie
4. wipe, ripe
5. fine, dine

**Page 42**

**Page 43**

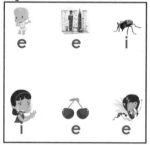

**Page 44**
1. blue
2. flute
3. tube
4. mule
5. cube
6. glue

**Page 45**
1. mule
2. cube
3. flute
4. glue
5. blue

**Page 46**

e   e   i

i   e   e

**Page 47**
1. fry
2. July
3. city
4. fairy
5. cherry

**Page 48**

**Page 49**
1. The hen is on the egg.
2. The frog is on the log.
3. A toad is in the boat.
4. A cube is on a mule.

**Page 50**
1. cupcake
2. starfish
3. doorbell
4. raincoat
5. ladybug

**Page 51**
1. doghouse
2. snowman
3. catfish
4. football
5. rainbow

**Page 52**
1. sailboat
2. bedroom
3. pancake
4. sandbox
5. seashell
6. peanut
7. spaceship

**Page 53**
1. backyard = back + yard
2. baseball = base + ball
3. butterfly = butter + fly
4. backpack = back + pack
5. goldfish = gold + fish

**Page 54**
1. I'll → I will
2. we're → we are
3. it's → it is
4. weren't → were not
5. I'm → I am

**Page 55**

I'll ─ were not
won't ─ you will
I'm ─ I will
it's ─ will not
weren't ─ it is
you'll ─ cannot
they're ─ do not
don't ─ they are
can't ─ I am

# Answers

## Page 56
1. din|ner, din, ner
2. kit|ten, kit, ten
3. mit|ten, mit, ten
4. hap|pen, hap, pen
5. pup|pet, pup, pet
6. zip|per, zip, per
7. muf|fin, muf, fin
8. but|ton, but, ton

## Page 57
1. ple
2. mer
3. ten
4. za
5. py
6. low

## Page 58
1. nap|kin, nap, kin
2. bas|ket, bas, ket
3. doc|tor, doc, tor
4. pic|nic, pic, nic
5. mon|key, mon, key
6. win|ter, win, ter
7. sis|ter, sis, ter
8. pen|cil, pen, cil

## Page 59
1. wal
2. tur
3. tur
4. roos
5. mon
6. pen

## Page 60
1. cats
2. kite
3. drum
4. roses
5. cakes
6. frogs

## Page 61
1. gifts
2. maps
3. kites
4. books
5. cups
6. dogs
7. birds
8. cakes

## Page 62
1. es
2. es
3. es
4. s
5. s
6. s
7. es
8. es

## Page 63
1. leaves
2. loaves
3. knife
4. calves
5. wolves
6. elf

## Page 64
1. teeth
2. geese
3. children
4. oxen
5. women
6. mice

## Page 65
1. feet
2. teeth
3. children
4. geese
5. men
6. ox
7. fireman
8. person
9. mouse
10. woman

## Page 66
1. mailbox
2. raincoat
3. toothbrush
4. butterfly

## Page 67
I will → I'll
it is → it's
they are → they're
we are → we're
you are → you're

1. cats
2. roses
3. dresses
4. women
5. oxen
6. leaves
7. peaches
8. knives
9. mice
10. feet

## Page 68
1. round
2. just
3. four
4. fly
5. old
6. sleep

## Page 69
1. fly
2. four
3. old
4. sleep
5. round
6. just

## Page 70

1. very old
2. went to sleep
3. just think
4. four of them
5. is round
6. can fly

## Page 71
1. fly
2. four
3. round
4. just
5. old

## Page 72
1. sing
2. green
3. open
4. over
5. stop
6. give

## Page 73
1. green
2. open
3. over
4. stop
5. give

## Page 74
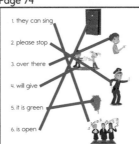
1. they can sing
2. please stop
3. over there
4. will give
5. it is green
6. is open

## Page 75
1. stop
2. give
3. open
4. sing
5. green

## Page 76
**Fruits:** lemon, apple, orange, grapes
**Vegetables:** corn, carrot, broccoli, lettuce

## Page 77
1. olive
2. dog
3. yarn

## Page 78
**Summer clothes:** shorts, sandals, swimsuit
**Winter clothes:** earmuffs, scarf, mittens

## Page 79
1. five
2. tiger
3. bat

## Page 80
**Flowers:** daisy, rose, tulip, pansy
**Trees:** pine, oak, palm, willow

## Page 81
1. balloon
2. key
3. kite

## Page 82
1. old
2. stop
3. sing
4. just
5. over
6. green
7. open
8. fly

## Page 83
1. Things you find in the kitchen
2. Things that are toys
3. Things that are insects
4. Things that can hop

## Page 84

## Page 85

## Page 86
Trees Are Homes

## Page 87
A Special Cake

## Page 88
People make wishes.

## Page 89
Buster likes to do many things.

## Page 91

# Answers

## Page 93

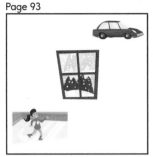

## Page 95
1. false
2. true
3. false
4. true
5. true

## Page 96
**3** Mom waters the garden.
**2** Kate and Tim plant the seeds.
**1** Dad digs up the dirt.

## Page 97
**1** Grandma and Juan stop at the baker's.
**3** Juan eats a peach.
**2** Grandma buys some flowers.

## Page 98

## Page 99

## Page 101

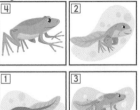

## Pages 102–103
1. tired
2. excited
3. sad
4. happy

## Pages 104–105
1. a
2. b

## Pages 106–107
1. a
2. b

## Pages 108–109
1. b
2. a
3. b

## Page 110
a. Milk the cow and feed the chickens and pigs

## Page 111
**Suggestion:** a puppy

## Page 113
**Fact**
There are seven days in a week.
Earth has only one moon.
Roses come in many colors.
**Opinion**
Orange juice tastes good.
Blue is the prettiest color.
Dogs are the best pets ever.

## Page 115
1. Opinion
2. Fact
3. Fact
4. Fact
5. Opinion

## Page 117
Main idea: Yoli Goes Shopping
1. c
2. b
3. a
4. a

## Page 118